Merlin's Magnificent Magic Shop

by

Carl Taylor

Cornelsen

Merlin's Magnificent Magic Shop

von

Carl Taylor M.A., Maidencombe, Devon

Illustration

Robert Broomfield, Tunbridge Wells

Zu dieser Ausgabe gehört:
Cassette, Best.-Nr. 59510

Cornelsen online http://www.cornelsen.de

1. Auflage Druck 16 15 14 13 Jahr 06 05 04 03

Alle Drucke dieser Auflage sind inhaltlich unverändert
und können im Unterricht nebeneinander verwendet werden.

Druck: Saladruck, Berlin

ISBN 3-464-05331-8

Bestellnummer 53318

Gedruckt auf säurefreiem Papier,
umweltschonend hergestellt aus chlorfrei gebleichten Faserstoffen.

Introducing ...

Merlin the magician

and his magnificent assistant

Dr K Nickel

Other characters

Laura

Kevin

Liz

Dave

Sandra

Richard

The speaker/reporter

(Outside Merlin's house. One of the pupils is the speaker.)

People often look at this funny house. It isn't like a normal house. The rooms are, well, in funny places. The dining-room is over the kitchen. The kitchen is over the living-room. The bathroom is upstairs. The rooms and everything in them are all different colours, too. There are stairs inside, of course, but there's a ladder outside, too. People say that a magician lives in the house, but they sometimes see a rabbit. The rabbit comes out of a window downstairs and climbs up the ladder to the bathroom. It's very funny. (*The speaker goes up to the door.*) A lot of people want to know who lives in the house. Let's see who lives there.

Scene one

(*The speaker is now a reporter. He knocks on the door and Merlin opens it.*)

Merlin: Hallo. What do you want?

Speaker: Good morning. I'm a reporter from the *Hatfield News*. You've got an interesting house. When I talk about it with my friends, they always ask me, "Who lives there?"

Merlin: Me.

Speaker: Yes, and I say, "A magician lives there." Tell me, is that really your job? Are you really a magician?

Merlin: Am I what? Am I really a magician? Wait here. Don't go away. (*Goes inside the house and comes back with a wand)* Do you know what this is?

Speaker: It's a magic wand.

Merlin: Very good. Now look. Abracadabra! You are now a cat!

(*The speaker starts to bark like a dog.*)

Merlin: (*Shouts*) Dr K! Dr K! Another mistake. (*The speaker runs from the house. Dr K comes from inside the house.*) That reporter should be a cat, not a dog. I don't understand it.

Dr K: That's nothing. Look at me. I'm a rabbit. And I should be a normal person. I'm your assistant.

(*Inside the house*)

Merlin: This is terrible, Dr K. I don't understand it. My magic isn't working. What can we do? I think I need a new wand.

Dr K: I'm hungry, Merlin. It's your turn to cook today.

Merlin: Here, have a carrot.

Dr K: I don't want a carrot.

Merlin: All rabbits eat carrots.

Dr K: But I'm *not* a rabbit.

Merlin: Of course you're a rabbit.

Dr K: I'm only a rabbit because your magic isn't working. I'm your assistant. Remember?

Merlin: Yes, of course.

Dr K: And I'm still hungry.

Merlin: And we've got no food in the house?

Dr K: Nothing.

Merlin: Where's my wand? Am I Merlin, the great magician, or not? Watch this. Abracadabra! Here is the food.

Dr K: Nothing. It isn't working, Merlin.

Merlin: (*Again, louder*) Abracadabra! Food! Here on the table! Now!

Dr K: Oh Merlin, you do your magic every day, but nothing happens. I think you should give away your wand and magic books and look for a job.

Merlin: Look for a job? What can I do? I'm a magician.

Dr K: But who wants a magician when he can't do magic?

Merlin: You're right, Dr K. (*Suddenly*) I've got an idea. *You* can go to work.

Dr K: I'm a rabbit. Remember? Rabbits don't have jobs. They sit in cages and eat carrots.

Merlin: I've got another idea.

Dr K: And what is it?

Merlin: It's very good.

Dr K: Well, tell me.

Merlin: It's a fantastic idea.

Dr K: Tell me. I can't wait to hear it.

Merlin: "Merlin's Magic Shop."

Dr K: It's silly. (*Pause*) But I like it.

Merlin: Why is it silly? We can write lots of invitations. All the children and their parents can come. We can do tricks and magic. We can make lots of money.

Dr K: How can you have a magic shop when you can't do magic? And we haven't got a room.

Merlin: We can use your room. You don't need it.

Dr K: How can you say I don't need it? Of course I need it.

Merlin: You're a rabbit. Rabbits don't have rooms with beds. You can have a cage in the garden.

Dr K: And you don't need your magic books and all those things in the library. A cage in the garden. How can you say that?

Merlin: I'm sorry, Dr K. I'm just a crazy old magician. Oh, dear. Now you're angry with me. What can we do? We've got no food, no money, no magic. Just a silly magic wand and lots of old books. You're right, I don't need them. I don't want to see them again.

Dr K: (*Jumps up and down*) I've got an idea. Let's open "Merlin's Magnificent Magic Shop" like you say. But we needn't do magic. We can sell everything. What do you say? (*Laughs*)

Merlin: Sell everything?

Dr K: Yes. Give me some paper and a pen. Let's make the sign for the door.

Merlin: No. Dr K, stop! (*Dr K doesn't stop.*)

Scene two

Laura: (*Knocks on the door*) Hallo. (*Sees Dr K*) Oh, hallo. There's a big sign outside. "Merlin's Magnificent Magic Shop." Can I come in? Is your shop open?

Dr K: Oh yes, we're open.

Merlin: No, we're not.

Laura: Who's that?

Dr K: Oh, he's my partner, but don't listen to him. We're open. Come in, come in. My name is Dr K Nickel.

Laura: I'm Laura. (*Looks at the different things*) I like this book. It's nice. It must be very old.

Dr K: It is *very* old. And it is very interesting. You can learn to do magic with it.

Laura: Really? How much is it?

Merlin: (*Shouts*) You can't buy it!

Laura: I don't understand.
Outside it says "Merlin's Magic Shop" ...

Dr K: Merlin is right. You can't buy it. But you can have it. I'm giving it to you. It's a present.

Merlin: (*Shouts*) She can't have that book. That book is from my old, old, old, old, very, very, very old Uncle Rudolph.

Dr K: Don't listen to him. He's just a silly old magician.

Merlin: It has got the best magic in England. I'm sorry. You can't have it.

Laura: Perhaps I should leave. I think your partner is very angry. You can have the book back.

Dr K: No. I'm also a partner here. I'm your partner, Merlin. Isn't that right?

Merlin: That's right, Dr K.

Dr K: Well, I am the owner of half of this shop.

Merlin: Correct.

Dr K: So I can give away my half.
(*Merlin takes the book and hides it under his coat.*)
You can have the book, Laura. (*Shouts*)
Merlin, where is it? I can't find the book.

Merlin: (*In a chair*) I don't know. I'm asleep.

Dr K: You've got it. Give it to me, Merlin!

Merlin: I'm asleep. Can't you see?

Dr K: Where is it?

Merlin: I don't know what you're talking about.

(*Laura leaves.*)

Dr K: (*Finds the book*) Here it is. (*Sees that Laura is not there*) Oh, it's too late. What a pity. She is so nice.

Merlin: She is *what*? When she comes again, do you know what I will say? Hallo, Laura. I've got a present for you today. A nice little rabbit in a cage. Isn't he a nice pet? Give him a nice big carrot every day. But don't bring him back.

Dr K: But I like her, Merlin.

Merlin: Perhaps she doesn't like you. I've got a new idea. Bring the sign here. (*Dr K brings the sign.*)

Merlin: Take the last letter away from the last word.

Dr K: You're the magician. You do it. Abracadabra ... you know.

Merlin: This isn't magic. Take the last letter away. (*Dr K takes away the "p".*) Now write the fourth letter from the end of the alphabet.

Dr K: The fourth letter from the end of the alphabet. A - B - C ...

Merlin: From the end!

Dr K: Z - X

Merlin: Y!

Dr K: Why "y"? (*Reads*)
Merlin's Magnificent Magic Shoy.

Merlin: Don't ask me why "y". It isn't "y", it's "w".

Dr K: Merlin's Magnificent Magic Show.
(*Sees the book of magic*) I don't like the idea.
I must go and find Laura.

Merlin: Why?

Dr K: I want to give her this book. She can practise some magic and perhaps she can help me. Perhaps I can be a normal person again. And when she sees that I'm not a silly old rabbit, ...

Merlin: Stop. Wait a minute. I've got another idea.

Dr K: What?

Merlin: I've got something for you.
Something from my old, old, old, old ...

Dr K: I know, very old uncle. Come on, hurry up.

Merlin: ...very old Aunt Agatha.

Dr K: Really?

Merlin: Yes, but I must find it first. Wait a minute.
(*Starts to look in different places*)

Scene three

(*Kevin, Liz, Dave and Sandra come in.*)

Kevin: Hallo, Merlin. Hallo, Dr K.

Merlin: Hallo, boys and girls. It's nice to see you again.

Dr K: Go away. We're busy.

Merlin: Come in, come in. Don't listen to Dr K. But why are you here now? Why aren't you at school?

Liz: We're on holiday.

Merlin: Is it summer again so soon?

Dave: Yes, we can come here every day, Merlin, and visit you.

Dr K: How often?

Dave: Well, every second day.

Dr K: Come on, Merlin. You've got something for me. What is it? (*Takes a book*) Is it this?

Sandra: How is Dr K?

Merlin: He's all right.

Dr K: Be quiet and sit down! Come on, Merlin. It's important.

Merlin: Dr K is in love!

Liz: In love? Who with?

Merlin: Her name is Laura.

Sandra: Oh, I know Laura.

Dr K: She's so nice.

Merlin: (*Laughs*) He wants to give her half the house.

Dr K: Half the house? One silly old book. That's all.

Sandra: Poor Dr K.

Dr K: What do you mean, "Poor Dr K?"

Sandra: Well, you see, Laura is only interested in Richard.

Merlin: Who's Richard?

Kevin: You don't know Richard? He has got a rock band with some friends from school. Richard is the singer and he plays the flute, too. He thinks he is the greatest. You can hear him at the youth club disco on Friday evening.

Merlin: (*Thinks*) So Laura is only interested in Richard. We must help Dr K. It's time for some magic. (*He starts to look again.*) Now where is it? (*He finds a box.*) Here it is. (*Merlin takes a pair of very big glasses out of the box.*) Look at these. They're magic glasses. When you wear these glasses, everybody falls in love with you.

Dr K: Everybody?

Merlin: Everybody.

Dr K: I don't believe it.
(*Merlin wears the glasses.*)

Merlin: Do you love me, Liz?
(*Makes a sign that she should agree*)

Liz: Yes. I love you very much, Merlin.

Merlin: (*Gives them to Dr K*) And you, Sandra?
Do you love Dr K?
(*Makes another sign that she should say yes*)

Sandra: Oh yes. He's my favourite rabbit.
I love him so-o-o much.

Dr K: I want them, I want them! I must have these glasses! (*Runs away*)

Merlin: Where are you going?

Dr K: I must find Laura.

Scene four

(*Dr K sees Laura and runs up to her.*)

Dr K: Hallo, Laura.

Laura: Oh, hallo, Dr K.

Dr K: (*He is shy.*) What are you doing, Laura?

Laura: Well, it's a nice day and I'm walking through the park.

Dr K: Yes, I can see that. Where are you going?

Laura: Why?

Dr K: Do you want to come to the shop with me? We can look at some more things.

Laura: I don't know. I haven't got much time, Dr K.

Dr K: Merlin isn't there. (*She doesn't answer.*) Oh, Laura, I've got another present for you. (*He gives her the glasses.)* Here, look at these glasses.

Laura: They're very nice.

Dr K: They're magic glasses.

Laura: They're what?

Dr K: They're magic glasses.

Laura: Don't be silly, Dr K. You can't have magic glasses.

Dr K: Really. When you wear them,
everybody loves you.

Laura: (*Laughs and wears the glasses*)
It isn't possible. But they're very nice. I like them.

Dr K: (*Suddenly*) Wait! (*He thinks.*) Wait. That's wrong!
Help! No, you can't have the glasses.
No, you mustn't wear them. *I* must wear them.
It's a mistake. (*He tries to take them back.*)

Laura: Dr K! What *are* you doing?

Dr K: I must wear the glasses! It's a mistake! I ...

Laura: (*Suddenly sees Richard*) Oh, look. There's Richard. Do you think he can see me? (*shouts Richard!*)

Dr K: (*Jumps up and down in front of her*) No. Richard mustn't see you!

Laura: Dr K! He can't see me. You're in the way. Please go away.

Dr K: No. *I* must wear those glasses. I'm so silly. Oh, Merlin, help me!

Richard: (*He sees Laura and comes to her.*) Hallo, Laura. (*He stops.*) You look, ... really beautiful today. I ... (*They walk away together.*)

Dr K: Oh, no ...!

Scene five

(*Back in Merlin's house*)

Liz: Poor Dr K. Do you think he knows that the glasses are only a trick?

Merlin: Who says they're only a trick?

Sandra: But it isn't fair, Merlin. I hope Laura doesn't laugh at him when he shows her the glasses.

Merlin: I hope he remembers that *he* must wear them. (*Laughs loudly*) Just think - Laura wears them and Richard sees her. (*Laughs again*) Isn't that funny? (*The others don't laugh.*)

Kevin: No, it isn't funny, Merlin.
And I hope Laura doesn't laugh at him.

Dave: You know that Dr K likes Laura.

Merlin: Yes, well, mmm, well, I'm sorry.

(*Dr K runs into the house, very upset.*)

Dr K: Merlin! Merlin!

Sandra: Dr K!

Dr K: She's with Richard.

Liz: Oh, Dr K!

Dr K: She's wearing the glasses. And Richard is with her. He ... he ... Oh, no!

Kevin: What is it, Dr K?

Dr K: You should hear him! "Oh, Laura, you're so beautiful. Laura ... Mmmm, I love you ... Mmmm ... Oh, Laura ..." It's terrible. What can I do?

Merlin: We need more magic.

Dr K: No! please! No more magic! I don't need magic. I need help.

Merlin: I've got the right thing for you now, Dr K.

Dr K: But no tricks!

Merlin: No tricks, Dr K. Liz, Sandra, you must help me.

Liz: All right, Merlin.

Sandra: All right, Merlin.

Merlin: What can you see here?

Liz: A box.

Merlin: Good. Now open the box. What's inside?

Sandra: Another box.

Merlin: And what's inside that?

Liz: Another box. ... And another box ...

Sandra: And another box!

Dr K: And it's a trick. There's nothing in those boxes. You ... you can't help me, Merlin.

Sandra: (*She opens the last box.*)
Oh, there's something here. It's a flute.

Dr K: A flute? I can't play the flute.

Merlin: That is my old, old, old, ...

Dr K: Very old, I know.

Merlin: ... very old Uncle Rudolph's flute.

Dr K: Oh no, another silly story.

Kevin: Tell us, Merlin, please.

Dave: Yes, Merlin. Please tell us about the flute.

Merlin: Well, this is a magic flute. When you start to play it, it makes very beautiful music. And when you hear the music, you want to listen to it all day. You can't go away from it.

Dr K: But I can't play the flute. What can I do with it? And if Richard gets it, I will never see Laura again.

(*The lights go out and somebody plays the flute. When the lights go on again Richard comes in with Laura.*)

Laura: Hallo, Dr K. Hallo, Merlin. (*She sees the two girls and boys.*) Hallo. Can we come in?

Richard: That's a beautiful flute. I was outside with Laura on the street. The music is beautiful. Is it this flute here?

Dr K: No. It's ... it's a record.

Merlin: It's my flute. My name is Merlin. And you must be Richard.

Richard: Yes. How do you know?

Merlin: I'm a magician and magicians know these things. (*Laughs*)

Richard: Can I try the flute? I play one like this in the band.

Dr K: No. You can't play it. It's broken.

Merlin: Don't listen to him. It's all right.

Richard: It's really very nice. Can I buy it?

Dr K: I'm sorry. We don't sell things.

Merlin: But Dr K, you want to sell everything.

Dr K: No, I'm sorry. I can't sell that flute.

Merlin: Are we partners, Dr K?

Dr K: Y - e - s.

Merlin: Am I the owner of half of this shop?

Dr K: Y - e - s.

Merlin: So I can sell my half. And that flute is ...

Dr K: ... in my half!

Merlin: It's in my half!

Dr K: My half! It's in my half!

Merlin: No, it isn't!

Richard: Don't argue, please! I don't want the flute.

Merlin: Wait a minute, wait a minute.
You don't want the flute? Don't you like it?

Richard: Yes, of course. It's beautiful.

Merlin: It's a very special flute. Only a special person can play it. And when other people hear the music ...

Sandra: Oh, Merlin, stop, please. Think of poor Dr K.

Merlin: (*Doesn't listen*) This flute is for you, Richard. You can have it. It's a present from me!

Dr K: Oh, no! (*Falls down*)

Richard: Thank you, Merlin. That's very good of you. But I don't think your partner is very happy.

Merlin: He's all right. Take the flute. Please.

Richard: (*Takes the flute*) Thank you again.
(*Laura and Richard leave. The children are very angry.*)

Liz: Merlin, that's not fair.

Dave: No, Merlin. You're not very nice.

Liz: Poor Dr K!

Merlin: Wait. Can I finish my story about my old, old, old, very old Uncle Rudolph's magic flute? Can I finish it, please?

Kevin: Go on.

Merlin: (*Laughs*) It's a very special flute.

Kevin: We know that.

Merlin: It's a magic flute.

Sandra: Yes! Go on.

Merlin: Well, you see, when you play it, you can't stop.

Dr K: (*Sits up*) You can't stop?

Merlin: You can only think of the flute and its music.
You play the flute all day and every day.
And soon your friends leave you because they think you're boring.

Dr K: (*Sits up*) You can't stop?

Dave: Your friends leave you?

Merlin: When the magic starts Richard will play and play and he will have no time for Laura.

Dr K: And Laura will leave him? I don't believe you!

Scene six

(*Laura is waiting for Richard.*
He is practising inside a room with his band.)

Richard: Hallo, Laura. I'm sorry I'm late.
Do you know what? Merlin's flute is fantastic.
We're practising a new song and it's just
the right thing. I can't stop. I want to play
and play and play.

Laura: Really? Where are we going this afternoon?

Richard: Oh, Laura. I'm sorry. I'd like to go with you now,
but I can't. I want to finish the song. Why not
come in and listen?

Laura: It's boring. I just sit there and do nothing.
Who wants to sit and listen to music when it's so
nice outside?

Richard: The music is important, Laura.

Laura: And I'm not?

Richard: Yes, of course you are. But I can't stop now.

Laura: It's a beautiful day. We can go to the lake and
swim. If you go back to the band, what can I do?

Richard: You can still go to the lake and swim.
You've got lots of friends.

Laura: I don't want to go with my friends.
I want to go with you.

Richard: I can't come. Don't you understand?

Laura: You don't want to go with me. You only think of your silly flute and your silly band. I don't want to see you again. You can play your flute all day. It's boring. And you're boring and I don't think your band is very good. Your music is boring, too.

Richard: Laura! Well, ... if you don't like it, don't listen to it! And you're right. I don't want to go out with you. I want to play my music and play the flute. All day.

(*Laura walks away. Richard goes back into the room. We hear the flute again. Merlin and the children arrive.*)

Merlin: See, the magic is working. (*He's very happy.*) Ha, ha! Now it's time for Dr K. Let's go!

Scene seven

(*Merlin and the two boys come into the house. The two girls are also inside.*)

Dave: Where's Dr K?

Kevin: We've got some good news.
It's over between Richard and Laura.

Liz: So soon?

Merlin: My magic is *very* good.

Sandra: Dr K is in his room.

Liz: And he doesn't want to come out.

Merlin: Silly old rabbit. And we're trying to help him.
(*Shouts*) Dr K!

Dr K: (*Shouts back*) Go away.

Merlin: Dr K, listen. It's over between Laura and Richard.

(*Dr K runs into the room.*)

Dr K: Say that again.

Sandra: It's over between Laura and Richard.

Sandra: She doesn't like him now.

Kevin: Richard only wants to play his flute.
He can't stop!

Dr K: Where is she? I must find her.

Merlin: Wait! (*Dr K stops.*) You're still a rabbit, Dr K.
I think you should be a human being again first.
She will like you better.

Dr K: That's right! Where's that book of magic?
I must give it to Laura. Perhaps she can learn
the magic and ...

Merlin: Stop! Who's the magician in this house?
(*Makes a sign to Kevin*)

Kevin: You are, Merlin.

Merlin: Thank you. (*To Dr K*) I'm the magician.
And in this little bottle ... (*Takes a bottle*)
I've got some magic pills.

Dr K: I don't want them.

Merlin: Take these pills, Dr K.
And you'll be a normal person again.

Sandra: It isn't a trick, Merlin?

Merlin: No, it isn't.

Dr K: I'm happy as a rabbit. I think carrots are fantastic.

Merlin: (*He puts the pills in a glass of water.*)
Take the pills, Dr K.

Dr K: No! I know your magic, Merlin. Two pills and I
will be a dog or a budgie. No, thank you.

Merlin: Come on, all of you. Hold him.

Kevin: We want to help you, Dr K. Really.

Liz: (*She looks through the window.*)
Laura is coming.

Dr K: Give me the glass. Perhaps she likes dogs and budgies. (*Dr K drinks the glass of water.*) Well ... what am I? Tell me before Laura comes.

Sandra: You're ...

Dr K: Yes?

Kevin: Dr K, you're ...

Dave: ... still a rabbit.

Dr K: Merlin, this isn't fair!

Merlin: I don't understand it. (*Looks at the bottle*) Wrong bottle. I'm sorry, Dr K. These pills make you ... ten metres tall. Where is the right bottle?

Liz: Merlin, Laura is almost here.

(*Suddenly the door opens and an old man comes in. Everybody stops and stands still.*)

Rudolph: Merlin!

Kevin: Who is that?

Rudolph: Merlin!

Merlin: Oh! It's my Great Uncle Rudolph.

Rudolph: Yes, it's me, Merlin. Sit down and listen to me.

Merlin: Yes...

Rudolph: I'm ashamed of you, Merlin. Look at you. You've got the same name as England's best magician. There are legends about him, books about him and what are you doing with his name? You're playing tricks.

Merlin: Yes.

Rudolph: You're a cheap magician. You're a clown. Do you know why your magic doesn't work, Merlin?

Merlin: No.

Rudolph: When you don't use your talents properly, they leave you. Your magic doesn't work, Merlin, because you don't use it to help people. You use it to play tricks.

Merlin: You're right, Great Uncle Rudolph. I'm sorry.

Rudolph: Now, Dr K, go into your room, wait thirty seconds and come out again.

Dr K: All right. (*He goes into his room.*)

Rudolph: And Merlin, you can come with me. It's time that you learn what magic is.

Merlin: All right, Great Uncle Rudolph. It's time to go.

(*Laura comes into the room.*)

Laura: Hallo, everybody.

(*Everybody is surprised.*)

Sandra: Oh, hallo, Laura.

Kevin: Hallo, Laura. What are you doing here?

Laura: Oh, I ... want to talk to Dr K. Is he here?

Merlin: Yes, he's here.

(*Dr K comes out of his room.
He is a normal person again.*)

Dr K: Hallo, Laura.

Sandra: Your magic works, Uncle Rudolph.

Laura: Oh ... hallo. You are ... different.

Dr K: Do you like me better now?

Laura: Oh, yes. (*Looks at the audience*)
Who wants a rabbit for a boyfriend?

Merlin: Well, I must go now.

Children: Oh, no. Please don't go.

Merlin: I'm sorry, I must go. Goodbye, Dave.
Goodbye Liz and Sandra. Goodbye Laura.
Goodbye, Kevin.

Children: Goodbye, Merlin.

Merlin: (*He pauses.*) Goodbye Dr K.

Dr K: And I must stay here without you?

Merlin: Yes. But I've got some good news for you. You are the new owner of the Magic Shop.

(*Merlin and Rudolph start to walk away.*)

Kevin: Merlin, please stay.

Merlin: I'm sorry, I can't.

Sandra: But we need you.

Merlin: I've got an idea. (*He takes the shop sign and he crosses out the "p" and writes a "w"!*)

Dr K: Merlin's Magnificent Magic Show.

Merlin: Yes, why don't you all write a play about an old magician? He lives in a very funny house with his assistant, Dr K. One day Dr K falls in love with a girl. Her name is Laura, but she only likes Richard. He is the singer in a rock band. So Merlin tries to help Dr K, but he doesn't help him really. He just plays lots of tricks and ...

(*Richard comes into the room.*)

Richard: I think it's a great idea.

Laura: Richard!

Sandra: What are you doing here?

Richard: And I want to write the songs.

Dr K: Brilliant. We can show the play to all our friends at school.

Rudolph: Merlin! It's time to go.

Merlin: Well, goodbye everybody.

Liz: But Merlin ... Wait.
We need you in the play. What should we do?

Merlin: It's only a play. One of you can be Merlin, all of you can do those silly little tricks. They're easy. I will come back when I can do magic properly. Goodbye.

Children: Goodbye, Merlin.

(*All wave as Merlin and Rudolph leave*)

E N D

Vocabulary

adv. = adverb, *pl.* = plural, *sing.* = singular, *sth.* = something

A **abracadabra** [æbrəkə'dæbrə] Abrakadabra
all [ɔːl] ganz
almost ['ɔːlməʊst] fast, beinahe
alphabet ['ælfəbet] Alphabet
also ['ɔːlsəʊ] auch
angry ['æŋgrɪ] ärgerlich, böse
as [æz, əz] wie
ashamed: (to) **be ashamed** [ə'ʃeɪmd] sich schämen
asleep: (to) **be asleep** [ə'sliːp] schlafen
audience ['ɔːdjəns] Zuhörer(schaft), Publikum
away: (to) **go away** [ə'weɪ] weg-, fortgehen

B (to) **believe** [bɪ'liːv] glauben
better ['betə] besser
boyfriend ['bɔɪfrend] Freund (eines Mädchens)
brilliant ['brɪljənt] toll, phantastisch

C **carrot** ['kærət] Karotte, Mohrrübe
character ['kærɪktə] Darsteller/in
clown [klaʊn] Clown
colour ['kʌlə] Farbe
(to) **come back** [kʌm 'bæk] zurückkommen
(to) **come in** [kʌm 'ɪn] hereinkommen
correct [kə'rekt] richtig, korrekt
(to) **cross out** [krɒs 'aʊt] ausstreichen

D **down** [daʊn] herunter, hinunter; herab, hinab

E **easy** [ˈiːzi] leicht
end [end] Ende, Schluss
everybody [ˈevribɒdi] jeder(mann)

F **fair** [feə] fair, gerecht
(to) **fall** [fɔːl] fallen
flute [fluːt] Flöte

G **glass** [glɑːs] Glas
glasses *(pl.)* [ˈglɑːsɪz] Brille
(to) **go away** [gəʊ əˈweɪ] weg-, fortgehen
(to) **go up to sth.** [gəʊ ˈʌptʊ] sich etwas nähern
(to) **go out** [gəʊ ˈaʊt] weggehen, ausgehen
greatest: **the greatest** [ˈgreɪtəst] der, die, das Größte

H **half** [hɑːf] Hälfte
(to) **happen** [ˈhæpn] geschehen, sich ereignen
(to) **hold** [həʊld] halten
human being [ˈhjuːmən ˈbiːɪŋ] menschliches Wesen

I **if** [ɪf] wenn
important [ɪmˈpɔːtənt] wichtig
interested [ˈɪntrəstɪd] interessiert
Introducing ... [ɪntrəˈdjuːsɪŋ] *hier:* Und jetzt präsentieren wir ...

J (to) **jump** [dʒʌmp] springen

K (to) **knock** [nɒk] klopfen

L **lake** [leɪk] See
last [lɑːst] letzter, letzte, letztes
legend [ˈledʒənd] Legende
loudly *(adv.)* [ˈlaʊdli] laut
(to) **love** [lʌv] lieben
in love with verliebt in

M **magnificent** [mægˈnɪfɪsnt] großartig, herrlich
metre [ˈmiːtə] Meter
mistake [mɪˈsteɪk] Fehler

N (to) **need** [niːd] brauchen
news *(sing.)* [njuːz] Nachricht(en), Neuigkeit(en)
normal [ˈnɔːml] normal, gewöhnlich

O **other** [ˈʌðə] anderer, andere, anders
over: (to) **be over** [ˈəʊvə] vorüber/zu Ende sein

P **pair** [peə] Paar
pause [pɔːz] Pause
(to) **pause** innehalten
perhaps [pəˈhæps] vielleicht
pill [pɪl] Pille, Tablette
play [pleɪ] Schauspiel; (Theater-)Stück
possible [ˈpɒsəbl] möglich
properly *(adv.)* [ˈprɒpəli] richtig
(to) **put** [pʊt] stellen, setzen, legen

R **really** [ˈrɪəli] wirklich, tatsächlich
(to) **remember sth.** [rɪˈmembə] sich an etwas erinnern

reporter [rɪ'pɔːtə] Reporter/in
right: (to) **be right** [raɪt] Recht haben

S **scene** [siːn] Szene
should [ʃud, ʃəd] sollte
(to) **shout** [ʃaʊt] schreien
show [ʃəʊ] Schau; Show, Theateraufführung
(to) **show** [ʃəʊ] zeigen
shy [ʃaɪ] schüchtern
sign [saɪn] Schild
so [səʊ] so
speaker ['spiːkə] Sprecher/in
special ['speʃl] speziell, besonderer
(to) **stand** [stænd] stehen
still [stɪl] still
story ['stɔːri] Geschichte
suddenly ['sʌdnli] plötzlich
surprised [sə'praɪzd] überrascht

T **talent** ['tælənt] Begabung
(to) **tell** [tel] sagen

U **upset** [ʌp'set] unglücklich

W **wand**: **magic wand** ['mædʒɪk 'wɒnd] Zauberstab
(to) **want** [wɒnt] wollen
was: **I was** [wɒz] Ich war
will (**'ll**) [wɪl] werde, wirst, wird, werden, werdet *(das Futur)*
without [wɪ'ðaʊt] ohne
(to) **work** [wɜːk] funktionieren